POEMS OF UNINHIBITED SENSUALITY

Emma Egbe

authorHOUSE®

AuthorHouse™
1663 Liberty Drive
Bloomington, IN 47403
www.authorhouse.com
Phone: 1-800-839-8640

First published by AuthorHouse   06/29/2011

ISBN: 978-1-4634-1478-8 (sc)
ISBN: 978-1-4634-1477-1 (hc)
ISBN: 978-1-4634-3470-0 (e)

Library of Congress Control Number: 2011910925

Printed in the United States of America

Dedicated to past, present and future lovers!

This particular book comes from the heart. I am dedicating it to past, present and future lovers. Every one of these men that have been in and out of my life have left something that has thought me a lesson and has helped me grow no matter how bad or good. Lovers just like everyone else that passes through our lives, make us stronger and wiser. They bring us joy or pain but in the end we are left with a little piece of them. They are part of the building blocks of our lives.

Sensuality is complete when served with a side of love.

Accolades

Young love

WAO! My hat off to you!!! I love it! Great write
Bernice Angoh (Author and health enthusiast)

Torn between two loves

OH! I FEEL YOU!!! but you know
the one who holds the future always wins :)
Bernice Angoh

Love and lust

Your poem can make a believer out of anyone, you're right,
there is sometimes a hint of lust, i guess we call that chemistry or
physical attraction?
Bernice Angoh

FORBIDDEN

This is an absolutely beautiful write

Bernice Angoh
Author or Lemonade Street and when a woman loves a man (Author house).

Nature

wao! wao! wao! I stand to applaud you. this is FINE writing!

 Bernice Angoh author of *when a woman loves a man* (Author house)

Change…..not

Ah! This brought tears to my eyes, this is what love does. It makes you beautiful!

Nature

I only wish I could put words together as well as you do. Beautiful and Dare I say sensual and steamy.

Cynthia Etonga
Lawyer and fashionista

Amazing way the words are put.
It stays on the sensuous side and does not go raunchy.
Very beautifully written and easy to read. Captivating to the point
where you want to keep on and find out what the next poem has
to offer.

Ako D
Master of the Arts

Good and satisfying sex comes as a result of total and complete liberation, the complete opposite of inhibition.

I am the last of 17 kids, 10 sisters and 6 brothers. Through my large family I have experienced just about every aspect of human character. Although I come from a very diverse family in terms of careers and education, my family has always placed special enfaces on the Arts. At a very young age my dad instilled in me knowledge by way of reading. I fell in love with books which included academic (such as the work of Shakespeare, T.S Elliot etc), history books, Novels (romantic, fiction and non-fiction etc). I have been reading novels since i was about 8 years old. My best subject throughout secondary and high school was always literature and i excelled at it and topped my class.

My knowledge of the world is also vast being that I have lived on 3 continents (Europe, Africa and America).

I have special causes that are dear to my heart and I am a member of Autism speaks. My son is autistic and I find this organization does a great job educating the public about the spectrum. I am also a member of March of Dimes organization. Anything we can do to better our kids today, secures our future and the continuation of "us".

I live in Maryland with my family. Being a mother is the toughest yet greatest accomplishment and joy of my life.

I use Poetry to capture my emotions in its purest
and most raw form.

My inspirations are pulled from everything around
me as well as a vivid imagination.

Contents

I REALISE THAT PEOPLE CONFUSE SEXY FOR SENSUOUS.

PLEASURABLE HEIGHTS

I like the way you comb my hair with your fingers
The way you kiss the back of my neck ever so softly
The sweetness of your inner lip drives me oh so crazy
The twirl of your tongue makes my toes curl.
Your tongue in my ear, makes me wet down there.
As i breathe in the scent of you, my body goes limp ready for you.
My insides ache, my legs part. Waiting for my king to take his throne.
You plunge into my abyss,
My head falls back,
My eyes roll back.
You plunge deeper in, a sound escapes my lips.
As you climb higher,
i am right by your side.
The world starts to spin.
I think i hear Zeus roar,
But that's just you as you soar.
High into the clouds you go,
Pulling me higher with you.
We break through the clouds together,
i think we just saw the heavenly lights.
Together we weightlessly float back to earth.
It feels like feathers when we land.
Sleep is a perfect ending, to the height we just attained.

YOU HAVE MY HEART

As i lay next to you while you sleep
I think of all the reasons i am here.
I love your strength
I love your dedication
I love your smile
Your sense of humor.
The way you watch me when i walk by,
Your hugs from behind,
Your hand rubs on my lower spine.
As i lay next to you now,
What i love most is your smell,
The rise and fall of your chest.
I watch you sleep and smile,
For you are never vile.
I debate to wake you or let you sleep.
I can't help it and lean in for a kiss.
My lips on yours,
Your lips part slowly.
hmmmmmm the warmth inside.
You pull me unto you,
My body comes alive.
Your kiss goes deeper,

The rhythm of my thighs is precise.
We grind and twine,
You are now "alive".
My stream begins to flow,
Good thing you are a thirsty one.
Your thirst drives you wild.
You begin to drink from my stream of life.
You drink again and again and again,
Until you glow with glee.
I am a happy giver,
You are a cheerful receiver.
You are not selfish,
And decide to replenish.
You give it back to me,
Again and again and again.
I can take no more,
My banks are about to overflow.
Bang!!!!!!!My dam walls burst open.
The shiver rivals a million bolts.
I see the stars.
This is what it means to be alive.
On top of everything else,
This is why you have my heart.

NATURE

Up in the woods
Held up in a cabin we lay
Looking into each others eyes
Hearing the owls and other night creatures sing.
Your hand caresses my face
My tiny hairs bolt up straight.
My body is transported in space
I can feel the warmth
The indoor temperature rises
Our energy is undeniable
The orchestra of creatures outside
Starts a melody for us
We move closer to each other
To enjoy the pleasures nature has to offer.
Your warmth is a divine pleasure
Which i will always treasure
My sense of feel heightens
Down below there moistens.
Your fingers find my core
My lava begins to rise
As you begin to explore,
My lava rises just a little more.
I am now very sure,

Nature's greatest marvels
Are in wet and dark caves.
I cry out for you to explore a little more.
Be my very own Columbus,
Loose your way and find it again.
My steam machine is rolling,
The creatures outside are howling.
My vision fades in and out
I feel the pleasure in my ears about to pop.
I try to speak but utter nothing but a whisper
I am at the edge of a cliff
Your tiny kiss on my earlobe takes me over the edge.
I scream as I fall,
Eyes closed and all.
Nature outside hears my call
And joins the chorus.
I don't drop as I thought,
But pleasurably float.
Engulfed in your arms,
Is the safest place I could ever be.
I am at peace with nature.
It gets quiet outside.
Nature and all its creatures,
Join us for a peaceful night.

I NEED A MAN

I need a man not a boy.
A divine creature of experience
Who has roamed the fields and the woods
One who has drank from unmentionable streams.
Rugged and strong
One that can align my spine better than a chiropractor
Rough hands against my skin to find every crevice
One wet behind the ears I do not want.
One with instincts of a wild boar,
Is what I adore.
One who can explore
With neither light nor map
One that can take down "cherries"
By hand, tongue or wand
One who knows how to
Pluck the ripe fruit
From the forest of womanhood
A trooper, fighter, artist, sculptor
One that can seek, be creative
Understands contours
And knows how to navigate his chosen land field
One who does not go by mans chosen "boundaries"

One with a trace of his ancestral early man instincts
A true man, a divine man
One that can make me
Cry as a wolf to a full moon
One that can make my dry sea banks overflow
One that can make my ears ring
One that can make me have
My very own heaven on earth

WHAT A SPECIMEN

What a specimen you are
Watching you always makes me smile
Your body glisters in the sun
You are every bit a man
One that has captured my heart

My love for you grows
Not by the day but by the minute
I think of the times we share
It blows my mind, this I swear
I must have done something right
For God to send me you at last

My heart is yours
As yours is mine
To you I give all that is me
You are my joy
You are my triumph
I wake up everyday
Glad to be by your side
I can't wait for the nights
To fall asleep in your arms

I searched the pond for too long
Many frogs I have kissed
My prince has finally come
With you I have no fears
You wiped away all my tears

Serenity does not even begin to describe how I feel
You bring me light, you bring me joy
You make me feel worthwhile.

TORN BETWEEN TWO LOVES

I love you both for different reasons
You light up my world
You are my rock
He stirs up a passion in me so strong
I can't stand my ground with him around
You are always loving and predictable
He is full of mystery that is so alluring
You make love to me like an English husband
He makes love to me like a Spanish outlaw on the run
Your love making is slow and precise
His love making is hot, heavy and filled with passion
You give me fantasy
He gives me ecstasy
I feel safe with you
I feel a rugged passion with him
Your eyes are bland
His eyes spit fire
You are my present and future
He is my past and present
This is tearing me apart
For I can not decide
It is killing me inside to have to let go
Of one of the great loves of my life.

SENSATION

I feel a burning sensation
Not a pain but an urge
One that only materializes when I have nothing
But you on my mind
I close my eyes and visualize the passion we shared last night
I can feel the warmth of your breathe on my neck
Your hand rubs on my inner thighs
Your pleasurable rubs on my womanly mounds
Your kisses so deep I feel you pull up my soul from within
My pleasure heightens as your kisses get lower
From my face to my "crater"
Warmth escapes as I open the gates
The expertise of your tongue can be rivaled by none
My body trembles with ecstasy from the pleasures from within
I faintly hear my mourns and they do not sound earthly
It can not be denied they could raise Lazarus from the dead
I feel my body elevate
We are intertwined as we climb
Up the spiral stairs we go
With a new pleasurable surprise at every turn
I pray this journey never ends

CURVES

You appreciate my curves
They make me a true woman
Your hands fill up with "all" of me
You love the cushiony filling of my thighs
The softness of my backside
The voluptuousness of my "topside"
My steadfastness when I "drive"
The reflection of my "behind" in the mirror makes you go wild
I close my eyes as I drive
My pleasure heightens as I ride
The neighbors call out from the sounds
The banging against the way has nothing on the acrobatics about to
happen
All inhibitions gone
All walls literally torn down
I feel my head explode
We cry out loud
Only a hyena at night
Can rival these cries.

PAINS OF LOVE

Rug burns
Grass stains
Metal poking my behind
Car seats laid down
Sand in my hair
Holding my breath under water
Consequences I bear to experience the pleasures of you
Cramping in my back
Cramping in my legs
Ringing in my ears
Countertop spot burnt into my thighs and behind
Worth all the pleasures you bring

YES

Yes, yes, yes oh baby yes
These are the sounds I love to hear from you
Yes, yes, yes oh baby yes are the best words my ears can hear
I love when you scream yes
I love when you growl yes
I love when yes comes from you in just a whisper
I love when you say oui like a French guy
Oui mon bebe oui
I love when you say dios mio mamasita
Your pleasure is my pleasure
My confidence is in your pleasure
My satisfaction is in your pleasure
De nada papi, de rien ma Cheri
Yes, yes, yes oh baby yes from you
Is wonderful music to my ears

SENSATIONS

Penetration, elation
Hunger, satisfaction
Burning desire
Body parts wet
Fingers and tongues everywhere
Bending, carving
Gymnastics, acrobatics
Huffing, puffing
Needs, wants
Satisfying desires
Hot, cold
Candle wax, ice
Cream, honey
Rubber toys
Heightened desires
You and I
Always together
Flying higher

FORBIDDEN

You are the forbidden
Not to be touched
Not to be lusted after
All because of the paleness of your skin
Like everything forbidden
You are delicious
Sensually scrumptious
It is impossible to stop after one bite
Your nectar gets sweeter with the peeing of every layer
I feel the burn, this must be my hell
I refuse to be denied of the pleasures you bring
Consequences I ignore, I am helpless to your charm
There is more I will like to explore
I know I am wide awake but you seem like a dream
I am ashamed of my broken defenses
I can't help wanting more
You make life perfect
In you I have found my oasis
The sweetness of your nectar has me wanting more
I feel like Eve in the Garden of Eden

BURNING DESIRE

The darkness in your eyes makes me tingle all over
The anticipation I see in them,
Tells me of the pleasures this night will bring
My chest constricts, I can't breathe
The anticipation of magic, transports me in time
You are my Greek God
I am your willful servant
Command and the pleasures shall be fully yours
My body is yours to explore
With galore and all
You give me feelings I can't ignore
Your magical wand is sure god made
I feel it grow as I press into you
I melt into you as your rod meets my bed of roses
The pleasures it brings are indescribable
The room gets hotter
By body is weightless
I can hear a locomotive pick up steam
To the movement of our hips
A cry escapes my lips
You catch it with a kiss
You raise your eyes to mine
Words are not needed to describe this moment
We connect in kiss
Everything is better when sealed with a kiss.

Valley of Pleasure

I am your queen of the Nile
Swim up and down as you please
No raft or canoe needed on this unrestricted stream
Enjoy all the pleasures of the God created valley
Wonders to be explored and had
Found no where else in the world
I'll be your Cleopatra
I'll be your Nefertiti
Life and civilization started right here
Take and eat of the fruits of this fertile valley
As your heart desires
May the juices run down your cheeks and chest
For I shall clean them with my tongue
Cleaning and pleasuring in one
For you are my god
These glorious lands are yours
To command and all.

PLEASURE

You make me come alive
Just by the magic of your smile
The twinkle in your eyes
Makes me smile
I watch you approach from across the room
Everyone else fades away
My spotlight is on you
Your stride rivals seabiscuit
The bulging of your front
Your muscular thighs
I try to hold your gaze
My eyes linger lower
I bite my lip to hold from crying out loud
My eyes slowly move back up as you approach
They lock with yours
I am transported in thought
My mind goes wild
I close my eyes so as not to betray myself
I know you are now near
Your scent forces my eyes open
We silently stare at each other
In your eyes I see the pleasures this night has to offer
I am the luckiest woman in the world
To call you my own.

Storm

Thunder and lighting rage outside the windows
Trees sway, branches break
Car alarms go off
We hear fire trucks in the distance
Police cars sounding their sirens
In here is serene
The peace and calm of us intertwined is beautiful
The glow of the burning fire against our skin
The shades of the burning candles against the walls
The glittering of the melted ice on your skin
Your lips upon my skin
The baritone of whoever is singing through the stereo
Brings me a sense of elation
A tiny tear rolls down my eye
The pleasures rattle my being to the core
I am blanked out by the height of my pleasure
I am thoughtless
I am speechless
I am fearless
My heart is whole
I am renewed
Just when I think you have given me all of you
You take me on a new adventurous journey
My Indiana Jones!!!!!!!!!!!!!!!

SEPARATION

I hate when you are away
The nights get extra long
I think of when you are here
My ache increases more
I know it has been just a day
My heart pains
I can't sleep
I have a burning desire
My hands roam all over "me"
Trying to trace the routes
You travel to bring me pleasure
I find your "truck stop"
I navigate with your touch from memory
Gently I begin
Then faster and deeper
I feel a mounting pleasure
The air my lungs hold
Burst out in pleasurable delight
My companion through it all
Is a picture of you in my mind
I fall asleep with a smile and you on my mind
Come back to me soon
And makes my nights warm and short.

THE OTHER SIDE

I have crossed the street to the other side
A man as wild and strong as a mustang
Has lured me across the street
All myths have been broken
None other can beat your rating
You have won the cup for your kind
Stamina, Agility, mobility, flexibility
And every other …lity you have shown.
I can't get enough of you
You are a master at your "craft"
Let the myths of my kind
Be perpetuated by the ignorant
I know best my peaces and cream ☺

HEALING

Your eyes melt my soul
Your body heals my eyes
Your touch brings me to life
Your arms bring the comfort of a sturdy branch
Your chest is a pillow where I lay my head
The rhythm of your heart is my lullaby
In your arms my body relaxes
My heart feels safe
My mind is at ease
My dreams are high definition
And crystal clear color
At this moment i pray the sun does not rise
So I can have this moment for life.

YOUNG LOVE

I remember our young love
So pure and innocent
To you I gave my all
Including my womanly gift
Recalling that night I begin to perspire
Under the bright moonlight
We crossed from this world into another
An ecstasy unknown to any other
Your gentleness and patience
Only rivaled the trace of your tongue
From the nape of my neck to my thighs
I could feel a storm brewing
The sound of the rushing waves approaching
A pleasure out of this world
Your fingers on my skin
Felt like Mozart on a piano
Your skills so undeniable
The pleasure you stirred in me
Made the moon turn red in my eyes
I crossed from childhood to adulthood
Under your spell
A beautiful and wonderful experience
A treasure in my heart
There it shall remain until the end of my time ☺

LOVE MAKING

Lovemaking is best with LOVE
Some can have it so blatantly
I prefer it served with a side of YOU
You make it better
You make it wetter
You make it last longer
You are the guru of my domain
I am under your spell
To you I give total control of my cells
Your scent elevates all other senses in me
Your scent is like oysters to my loins
One sniff of you and I say Ginseng who?
You are enough for me
You are more than enough for me
You are like Oxygen in my blood
You provide food to my body and soul
My scruffy little toffee
Or should I say my mighty warrior
You are the Zeus of this kingdom
The Poseidon of my waters
To you I bow in humbleness
My mighty godly warrior.

Words.......Not

To be good lovers
You have to communicate
We do not communicate by words
We talk by touch
You speak to me with your hands
Your hands says I love you
Your hands say I want more of you
Your hands say I can't get enough of you
I get you by your scent
It awakens me always from deep sleep
You heighten my senses
Your moans of pleasure say yes
Your moans say moreeeeeeee!!!!!
Your moans say don't stop
Your groans drown out my moans
Your groans tell me you like it
Your groans tell me you want it
This is how we communicate
We do not need words to speak.

You

My life is better because of you
You are a wonderful friend
My best lover
You allow me to be me
You accept my flaws and praise my strengths
You know just where to tickle to make me laugh
When I am sad
Your embrace always envelops me
Soothes me and brings me comfort
I will be incomplete without you
In you my strength grows
My smile glows
Without you my strength withers
You are my greatest desire
By your side I shall stay.
Even when apart
You always have my heart.

JOURNEY

I have been on a long journey
My journey to get to you
I have travelled though heavy forests
High mountains and low valleys
Been burnt by the sun
And shivered through the cold nights
On my journey to you
Dodged the teeth of hyenas
Poisonous snakes and wild dogs
On my journey to you
Now my heart is in your hands
I still have fears of being squished
I know I'll be alright
As long as you love me.

My weakness

Your stir a passion in me so great
My body cells seem to disintegrate
Making love to you is a mind blowing event
The ripples you cause on my body
Can't be handled by the weak
I am completely merged to you in spirit
The tickles of your fingers upon my skin
Can make a lady go insane
The heightened awareness you awake in me
Break down all the walls I had erected
You are the prince I dreamt of in my childhood
The twirl of your tongue digs out my spirit
From the run down alleys of my soul
I am unguarded against you
I have no defenses against you
When you touch me I come alive like a flower in spring
My juices flow like a stream
I can fight it no more
You are the one, None other compares
At the sight of you the butterflies within my womb begin to move
The sensation is ecstatic
One look from you I feel electricity powered by nothing
Burning sensations, burning desire
When you are around I have no power
I float towards you longing for your touch
My weaknesses are profound when you come around

LOVE AND LUST

Love and lust go hand in hand
I love and lust for you passionately
My lust for you aches my "lady parts"
My lust for you makes "drippy" in my underpants
I love the lust I see in your eyes
Behind the lust I see love
The rays of lust make the rays of love brighter
While I love your love
I need your lust
Your love is comforting
Your lust is satisfying
Lust without love is a drag
Love without lust is a bore
Love and lust go hand in hand and make it right
With love and lust my heart and groin are satisfied.

THE GARDEN OF ME

You never wither,
You always water
Shower my garden
You are my rock
That protects my heart of flowers from the bugs
You are my sunshine
That feeds my flower soul with much needed nutrients
You are my solid ground
Ground upon which my seeds grow
You are my manure
Upon which every good of me spurs
You are my wind
In which my beautiful flowers sway
You are my moonlight
In whose mighty light I shine
You are my vase
In which the indoor of me flourishes
With all of you by my side
I shall never die.

HOME COMING

Standing at the port
Waiting for your ship to dock
I feel the wind of the sea
And taste its saltiness in the wind
Mighty nights have come and gone
Without you where you belong
In my arms and in my bed
My body screams out loud like a throng
Sadly as I shiver in the wind
Waiting for you to get off the cursed ship
The one that sailed with you, away from me
I see your sandy colored hair
My insides take a dive
I try to move but I am planted by emotion
Tears run down my face
I see you smile and the sun climbs high in the sky
You walk over and sweep me in your arms
I bury my face in you and draw in a breath
A smell I have missed for a forth night
One that will end this very night

LUCKY ME

I shiver at the thought of you
I quiver in your wake
The insanity of you keeps me sane
The density of you keeps me grounded
In you I find my purpose
In your I find my realm
The realm to which I belong
Body, heart, mind and soul
I hear your whisper in the wind
I feel your touches in my dreams
The mornings come with your smile
The birds chirp to say hello
Your morning kiss is my coffee
Your kisses on my nose to get me to wake
Us watching the sunrise together
Make the day start right
I am very lucky to have your love
Love from my best friend.

My mind reader

You understand me like no other
You know when and where I like to be touched
You know just when to let me be
You are my mind reader
You know how to touch my soul in song
Your know my craves and fears
You are my mind reader
You know every pain
You know every joy
You understand my being
You are my mind reader
You understand when I want to be caressed slowly
You understand when I want it rough and wild
You understand when I want to be left alone
You are my mind reader
You hear me when I talk without words
You understand the talk of my body
You understand my desires and fantasies
You are my mind reader.
With you I need not fear to be lost in translation
You understand me before I speak
My one and only mind reader.

LOVE AND PAIN

Why does it hurt so badly?
How can something so beautiful shatter my heart?
They say it is better to have loved and lost
Than not at all.
I am not sure it is worth the pain
If it is supposed to bring me joy,
How come all I feel is sorrow?
If it was supposed to bring me laughter?
How come all I have left are tears?
Do I protect my heart from this pain
By not opening its doors to another
Or do I open the doors and hope a better someone
Knocks on it and brings me laughter and joy?

I think I am now healed
I try to open the doors of my heart to another
But the doors won't budge.
I try to push it open through the squeaking
But the doors won't open
What can I do to lubricate it so it opens?
I need it to open up to another
It heeds not to my wants but has a mind of its own
It stays in the shades and withers, wanting but not allowing those
pleasures to flow in.
How can I open the doors with the guarantee that no pain shall walk
in again?

THE ONE

You are the one
None other compares
I left I and went to 2, 3 and 4
Whatever the case, I always come back to I
There is nothing like the first
Everything else is but a duplicate,
A copy....not good enough
I tried so hard to make 2, 3 and 4 work
My mind always circles back to one
You are the **ONE**
My starting and ending point.

BROKEN DROUGHT

You broke my drought
My tap drips again
Thanks to your mechanical savvy
My thirst has been quenched
By the bounties of your reservoirs
Nothing tastes as good as your natural springs
Sexplore my valleys
Accept all of the fruits and joys it brings.
My plants flourish once more thanks to your bounties.

EFFECTS ON ME

Every time you come to my mind
A smile crosses my face
A tingly sensation runs across my spine
An electric sensation tinkles my "vault walls"

I LOVE YOU

I love you
Je t'aime
Ich Liebe dich
Te quiero
These are just a few ways
For me to tell you how I feel
Your touches on my skin
Make me scream Ave Maria
With you I attain unmentionable heights
You make my soul move
You make me feel whole again
You bring me joy and strength I have never known
You are my motivation.
I am lucky to be in love with my best friend
Je t'aime fort!!!!!!!!!!!!!!!!!!!

Second time

It is better the second time around

We learnt and grew from the first time

We know each others strengths and weaknesses

We know when to push and when to pull back

We know each others contours to bring ecstasy

The second time around comes with experience

We know to take it slow and enjoy the pleasures

No need to rush what you know will always be
There

We take It slow like the grown and sexy

WHY.....US

You offer me a warm embrace
To feel your love
I love the feel and warmth of your skin
Against my bare backside
As you crawl into bed after a hot shower
I arch my behind
To fit into the cradle of your groin
The comforting feeling
Brings a smile to my face
I press in backwards
As you press forward
 A sigh escapes you
A sigh of want and desire
I roll over and I am caught off guard
By the glow of the bedside lamp on your skin
You look heavenly I must admit
May the lord forgive me for the "evil" thoughts
That cross my mind at this moment.
The pleasures that come from this moment
Can not be out into words
Moments like this remind me why there is an "US"
I am content to have my sun rise and set with you.

SCRUMPTIOUS

I feel a drizzle within
I am ripening from within
Something stirs from deep within
From the inner most part which is unseen
And can only be felt by you.

One touch from you and I fell to pieces
I crumble under your touch
I crumble to delicious edible pieces
Pieces and crumbs to top
Your scrumptious banana split.

NOW OR NEVER

It is now or never for us
I need you now or never
I need you like my lungs need Oxygen
I need you like a car needs fuel to run
I need you like the clouds need water to form
It is now or never
My heart is constricted from want
It hurts from anticipation
I need you now or never
My urgency needs you now
Never is not an option

YUMMY YOU

I bite unto your earlobe
I sniff the curve of your neck
I run my hands on your torso
I lean into you from behind
I can't keep my hands of you
You have a mighty pull
Your fine skin and delicious smell
Always has me coming back for more

TANGO

Bubbles of perspiration
A result of us in Tango
We move with the flexibility
Of a dolphin swimming around in a pool
While we are in Tango
My limbs wrapped around yours
My face buried into your chest
Your arms on the my lower back
You pull me close to you
As we Tango
I am lost to the world
As I give my all to you
And let you lead me
As we Tango
I never want to let go
I love it when we Tango.

STRONG PULL

I fear loving you so strongly
I fear my heart will be lifted up to be smashed again
You are new territory for me
I feel like I have entered a field saturated with landmines
You are the unknown to me
A different kind of man
One with such a draw that I can't keep away.
I have always stayed amongst my kind
You are the cream to my coffee
I must admit cream makes it sweeter and better
I must admit I want to feel your hands all over me
I love it when you envelop me in your arms
When we lay there saying nothing
Just enjoying the pleasures of each others' company
I love to listen to the rhythm of your heart
It brings comfort to my being.

My crush

I watch you unnoticed
I imagine what it will be like to have you in my bed
I wish you will notice the way I look at you
I wish you will notice how I blush when you say hi
I yearn for you badly
I am crazy about you
I wonder what it will be like to spend a night in your arms
To feel your kisses upon my lips
I imagine having your hands roam all over me
And bring me pleasures I have long imagined
I get all sweaty when I am near you
My words get all rolled up on my tongue
I miss my steps when I walk into you
I get either tongue tied or gitty
Then I get nervous because I think I am being so obvious.
I hope I can develop the courage to let you know how I feel
If I can't have courage, I pray you notice how I feel.

YOUR TOUCH

I beg for you not to stop
I ask you to keep on
No other can do the things you do to me
You are the definition of a good lover
I love when you blow kisses on my skin
It makes parts of me as hard as a rock
And others as moist as a newly watered garden
All my senses go to pieces
When you do those marvelous things to me
You get my blood near boiling
MY heart beats so fast that I can hear it ring in my ears
I feel like I have left this world behind to a planet called pleasure.
All by the wonders of your touch.

FOREVER

With you I have discovered the true meaning of love
In my arms is where I wish you will stay
Belong to me I plead with you
I am head over hells in love with you
With you I know the essence of love
Together we have climbed the highest mountains of passion
I completely surrender myself to your will

Everyday I wake up to you as my light
I can't live without you
Life will be meaningless without you around
I want to show you how much I love you
By giving you the very best of me
You bring me such joy
The elation I feel with you is so wild
Be mine and mine alone
I am glad to have a love like yours everyday
On my bossom you can peacefully lay your head
May the rhyme of my heart claim your mind
May this be your resting place for ever
Forever with you is all my heart desires.

Independence day!!

Tonight is my 4th of July
You bring me the fire works
I want these sparks all year round
While others keep it for just one day
Today is my independence day
The day I am liberated by your touch
Red, white and blue
Are the colors of the stars I see when with you

Today I am free
Free from the bondage of boring love
You have made me a free woman
Today is my Fourth of July
My skies light up with the flashes
Of the fireworks you bring
Red, white and blue
Are the colors of the stars I see when with you.

CONQUEROR

You have pushed through the trenches of my heart
To find the core filled with love
You are the conqueror of my forest
With the flames of your mighty dragon
Bushes and trees burnt to ashes
The forest is all trimmed to your liking
Take over my land of pleasure
And build on it as your wish.

COMFORT

I love when you walk up to me from behind
And grab me in your bear hug
I lean into you and swim in the safety of your arms.
I feel safe and fear nothing when you are near.
 I love when we stay in bed just because
I love the days we stay in bed all day just because we want to
I love lazing in bed with you when the sun comes up in the sky
I love to lay my head on your chest and hear the morning crowd go
about their business.

WHILE YOU ARE GONE

I miss laying with you
My bed is cold with you gone
I can't get you off my mind
I miss you while I enjoy
The reminiscence of your smell on my pillow.
I can't get enough of you
You have stolen my heart
It is very hard for me when you are not around
I wish you were here for me to just lay next to you
I love watching you sleep when I can't
I miss having your body next to me.
I miss your kisses on my neck while I sleep
I smile at the thought of me playfully
Slapping your hand away as you grab on my behind
Causing a playful fight
Which always ends in a steamy make up session
While you are gone
I miss you dearly my love.

ALL YOU'LL EVER NEED

I am all the spice you need
Within me you can weep
May your waters flow though the contours
Of my tube to my crater
To the crater that holds life
Within my bosom
Lay all the pleasures you'll ever need.

RENEWED

You bring me joy
Joy in my heart and mind
What could I possibly give to you in return
I appreciate you that's for sure
I had reached my lowest when you came along
You picked me up from a bush of thorns
I have blossomed in your hands
My friends and family see the new light
That radiates from the very core of me
I appreciate you
You know just where to prick to make me smile
I walk around with the joys of you left on my skin
I wake up ready to face the days knowing you
Are there to catch me if I fall
I look forward to the days end
To come to you

Vixen ....Me

You are the stranger I picked out in the dark
You came out of the dark and brought light to my life
You make me feel like a vixen at the cinema
My confidence has been boosted by you
Loving every flaw of my humanly flesh
You devour me like a woman you paid for
Trying to get your every worth
While making me feel like a queen
Knowing that this marvelous man
Chose me amongst the millions available
Makes me feel very glorious!

FEELINGS

I feel a strange sense of being watched
Look up and my eyes meet with you far across the hall
I get a tinkle in my no- no zone
Could this be real?
A man's effect on me from a distance
I smile and look away and try to take a peak again
You catch me look and smile
I feel my legs go wobbly.
Is this love at first sight?
Who knows or cares
Love or lust?
Whatever it is, I sure can appreciate it.

LOVE ON THE DANCE FLOOR

I melt into you on the dance floor
My head on your shoulder and your arm around my lower back
We swerve to the beats of beautiful Caribbean music
We move around effortlessly
The energy between us is beautiful
The DJ deems the lights and we are transported out of here
As your arm moves up and down my back
I feel the very core of me cry to be touched.
We move into each other and become one
I can feel the excitement of you through the clothes
I smell my excitement
A scent only we can recognize
We sway in unison
I reach a peak just by the touch of your skin on the dance floor.
It feels like we've been hit by a million bolts
As we swerve together in unison
This is love on the dance floor.

ALL MY LOVE

I never knew I could love someone so strong
And then you came along
Now I understand what it means
To give your all
I feel a pain within when you are away
I give you my heart when you leave
And stay empty until you return
And place it in my chest again

Music

We dip our legs in the pacific
Watching the orange glow of the sun set
I feel close to you than anyone else
I shiver at the tiny wind
You move closer and bring me warmth by your embrace
The tranquility and flow of the waves
Signifies the co-existence of us
Peacefully clashing together in perfect harmony
Making beautiful music to the setting sun
I can live like this for ever.

NIGHTMARE

I cry out at night
I cry from the dept of my sleep
I cry out to you to love me again
To give me those feelings I so long for
I try to hold on to you but you move away
I wipe my eyes to see through the blurs
The blurs of the images of you
You keep moving away
I run up and try to catch you
You slip right through my hands
I feel a powerful kick in my chest
That's just the pain of watching you walk away
As I ache I cry out for you to stay
I try to run after you but I am plated on the spot
I feel wetness on my eyes and try to wipe
They are not my tears but kisses from you on my eyelids.
I come back to life and see you by my side in my bed
The pain evaporates; it was all just a dream
You pull me to you and reassure me
It was but a dream, never to come true.

FEELINGS

I hear your thoughts when you are not here
I feel your pain across state lines
When you worry, my heart hurts
My day goes right when you are glad
I feel your soul within my chest
We are synched as one.
I know that I have found my soul mate
We are one in spirit
We are attached across unseen twine
I need you to know
In me you have a friend
A partner in crime
One to wipe away your tears
One to stand by you when no other would
I beam with pride at your accomplishments
I reinvent myself every time just for you
I am whoever you want me to be when need arises
We have fun with my many characters
Others call me schizo, you and I know the deal
We are one body, mind and soul

ONCE MORE

You came to me like a thief in the night
One that came and stole my soul
You stole my soul with your kisses
You stole my being with your magic
You broke down my walls effortlessly
I perish into a pile
When you put your hands on my thighs
I feel no danger when you take me for a wild ride
There is no difficulty in our merger
Smooth riding, clear sailing
Tenderness is what you bring
You show me the pleasures of life
Life is beautiful once more
Who said life was over?
You have elevated me to infinity

ALL YOURS

Everything in the past is exactly where it shall stay
Here and now is just you and i
You touch me and I feel the love you have for me
I hold back, you tell me to let go
To trust my heart to you to keep save
You promise to cherish it until the end of time

YEAH ....RIGHT

You always walk behind me
I ask curiously why
You say to keep me save
And protect me from behind
This I find not to be true
I see how you watch me when I turn around unexpectedly
You blush at being caught
I must say I am flattered.
I swear you say........just making sure you are safe
All I can say while I laugh is YEAH ....RIGHT ☺

WEATHER COMPANION

Welcome cloudy skies
Welcome thunderous rain
While you shake the roofs and make us stay indoors
We love the sounds you make to drown out our thunderous games.
Roar some more, mighty skies
Join us in song as we cry out in pleasure
As we sing the songs of man
The songs that come as a result of mighty pleasures
Cloudy skies, thunderous rains
We thank you for keeping us indoors.

ONLY YOU

Under the waterfall in the simmering sun
I get to enjoy the exoticness of you
Instead of the wonderful tropics where we are
I admire the crystal glares the water makes on your skin
Right here and now I am captivated by your essence
I want to drink in all of you
To run my cup over

BOND

I am bonded to you
You are bonded to me
Together as one
We move about this world
Together in ecstasy and fantasy
Across the starts and the oceans
I feel you within my soul
I send love to you in my deeds
We were brought together by the cosmos
Looking up at the stars at night
I see you smile down at me
I close my eyes and feel your caress
By way of the star light upon my face
I feel your kiss on my lips by way of the wind
You feel me rub my hands up and down your staff
By way of the night breeze
You harden up thinking of my deeds
We are bonded as one far across the land
A bond so strong that can move across time.

Love, love, love

Some say a love like ours can not be real
They say a love this strong can not be true
I have decided to love you with all of me
As you have given me all of you
I love you honestly like a little girl loves
With purity and trust
They say I love stupidly without guard
Without protection for my heart
How can I love you genuinely if I guard up my heart
You love me with all of you and so I give it back to you.
I love you as you love me
Unconditionally with no reservation
I love you like a fool they say
You love me like a moron others cry
I love you, you love me
That's all that matters

NOT GIVING UP ON YOU

I am not giving up on you
I love you too dearly to give up
Whatever it is you are going through
Get through it and come back to me
We were about passion and truth
Then came the dark clouds
I see you though eyes like no other
I am not giving up on you

You say you were held by my leash
A leash of love and passion
One that was no issue until the dark clouds came
I refuse to give up on you
I will fight for you to come out of the shadows

Think of the love we shared
The joys we had
The laughter we created
I will find words to get to you
I will find magical formulae to make you hear me again
The magical formulae given to me by the most high
That rests right in the very heart of me being a woman.

CHANGE..............NOT

He asks me to change who I am
So he can love me again as he did before
He asks me to slim down my hips
The hips that give me the curves you so adore
He asks me to loose my curves and become a 2
You love me at a 10 or 12
You love me, hips and all
More landscape for you to explore you say
He asks me to take out my hair
Hair you don't mind me having
You like when I switch it up
He asks me to lighten my skin so I can look more appealing
to him and the mass he says
You love me with my milk chocolate glow
It shows I have been touched by the beautiful African sun
I dared to change myself to retain his love
I lost my hair he so loved from the stress
My waist line grew bigger from the stress as well
Which instead pushed him away
I lost sleep from worry and it affected my complexion's glow
he so wanted me to change
Now I have you and all the stress is gone

I have slimmed down from peace of mind
My skin glows once more
It radiates the love it receives from you
My hair, body and mind are peaceful once again.

CAMELEON WOMAN

I am your Amazon woman
To have and to hold
I reinvent myself every time for your pleasure
I am your secretary when you need me to be
I am your welder when you are in need of hand work
I am your glass blower when your glass needs to be blown
out
I am your dignified state lady when need be
To stand by you and command the respect of your peers
I am your mama to cradle you when you need to be rocked
I am a street lady for you once the lights dim
I am whatever you need me to be
As long as it brings you pleasure.

MYSTERY MAN

My dark handsome prince
You never stop
Strong as a mustang
With the horsepower to match
My very own Jason Bourne
Born to make me happy
I can't stop myself when I have your hands all over my body
You came from out of this realm
Came down with the mastery of things no other man can
compare
I intend to keep you right here.

FIRST KISS

Under the tainted bridge we stole our first kiss
Trickles of rain falling all around us
Held up in our own little space
Oblivious to the world around us
The sweetness of your kiss spurred the very depths of me

Scared and elated at the same time
I prayed the kiss will never end
I pressed myself to you in pleasure
And delighted in the moan that escaped you

Strange as this was for me being the first time
I was not scared knowing I had you to guide me through
The power of your kiss left an everlasting taste on my lips
One I can still feel and taste 'til this day.

SUMMER LOVE

I remember the summer I longed for you
You pushed me away
My heart shattered to pieces
I tried very hard to go on without you
Tried very hard and mended my bleeding heart

Four years later you came to my door step
Pledging your undying love for me
And asking for mine in return
I told you I had no love to give
My love was already with another

You called me uncaring
You called me cruel
You called me insensitive
That's exactly how I felt about you
Four summers ago.

Through the Pain

You did everything to stay by me
In spite of the odds against you
You were my rock through the trying times
You kept me sane with your love.
You made sure I believed in me
You told me I was beautiful on those days I felt like a troll
You made me know there is one person that will never turn
their back on me
That person was you
You cradled me through the dark days
And made me know the sun will shine again
You brought me food when I could not get myself out of bed
You pulled me into the shower when I could have cared less
You danced around silly to make me laugh
Laid in bed by me on those cold nights in the dark when I
did not want light
You cradled me through the stormy nights
Knowing I fear the dark
How can I fight the love I have for you in my heart
I shall always keep you in that spot
Right below my left breast.

DARK HANDSOME ONE

I remember when I first met you
The light in your eyes bore through my soul
My insides did a somersault at a creature
Made of gold
I saw you sweep a sensual look across my frame
I wondered if it was ok for me to do the same
I did anyway because I could not help not to
Sturdy as a horse, pretty as a Persian prince
Broad chest, strong arms
Tanned and toned
Looking so bold
Just a few things I made a mental note on
Maybe my mind is too wild
For I could see us intertwined
I closed my eyes as not to be betrayed
By the lust they portrayed
The beating of my heart picked up steam
I felt like I could not breathe
I literally had to catch my breath
And place my hand on chest
Just to make sure I was awake
Little seat bubbles formed on my nose
You walked up and asked me if I was alright

Even though at that moment I could not speak
I knew I had to make you mine to keep
Stuttering as I tried to speak
I offered my hand and a smile instead
Your kiss on the back of my hand
As you said hi
With the dark look in your eyes
Told me I had met the one
To bring me all the pleasures I have ever desired.

NOTES FROM AUTHOR

While the book is geared on sensuality, and the blossoms of love. It also shows that love can bring both joy and pain. You hear the cries or laments of love in some of the poems. While love is a powerful feeling that brings all kinds of joys, it is also the most powerful feeling that brings us pain, sorrow and tears. We can only guard our selves so much from the pains of love.

Keep in mind that once we get very guarded to avoid being hurt; we also prevent love from coming into our lives. So I will advise as my wise cousin Anthony Nana (Author of Timbuktu Chronicles, Aida and the chosen soldier: Author house publication) told me. No matter how you think love hurts also be willing to open yourself up to allow someone else to bring love again into your life. Besides new love, takes the old pain away.

EMMA!